Positive Discipline

How to Raise a Capable and Confident Child through Simple and Effective Techniques of Toddler Discipline

Kate Cartes

Table of Contents

Introduction

Positive discipline is a natural teaching tool that is based on three simple steps: Positive reinforcement, positive direction, and positive guidance. It teaches children to make better choices and can help them develop successful habits over the long term. People who implement positive discipline regularly have better relationships with their children and enjoy a closer bond. No matter how old you are, positive discipline can benefit your entire family. We believe that parents and schools are more effective when they apply positive discipline. With positive discipline, you teach your kids the way they should behave. You want your kids to learn from their mistakes and to make good decisions.

This book teaches you how to combine positive discipline with motivational coaching in the classroom. You'll use positive discipline once your child has been caught doing something wrong. Then, you can help them make a better choice in the future by showing them how their mistakes have consequences.

Positive discipline works for all ages of children, including preschoolers. This book will help you apply it in the classroom as well as at home. It covers many examples of what successful parents and teachers use to teach children.

CHAPTER 1:

Positive Discipline Principles for Your Family

Discipline is one of the most widely covered and controversial topics that appear in parenting books, blogs, and various other mediums. Social media is brimming with judgmental parents and non-parents who feel compelled to give their advice and insight. Try to bring in a judge-free mentality for this chapter because the Montessori discipline does spark a lot of controversies. Not only that, it preaches self-discipline, but it also preaches positive discipline and not encouraging your child.

Now, self-discipline is something we're all familiar with and is really something we expand on as adults. We learn the hard way we are responsible for our behavior, our reactions, and other elements of our life that until adulthood seems out of our control. Self-discipline, or the lack of it, is largely to blame for much of that teenage angst.

Diving into the positive discipline and the controversial element of encouraging your child or offering praise will take more than the brief touch on self-discipline. In this chapter, you'll find a variety of techniques largely regarded as positive discipline and have been found to build empathy and a cooperative relationship. The Montessori Method is not the only system or belief pattern that offers positive discipline. Many pediatricians and child psychiatrists also support Maria Montessori's foundation for positive discipline. It's worth noting now; positive discipline sounds a little backward. Most of us were raised with good old traditional negative discipline, which is as bad as it sounds. Both parents not only believe that that's normal but don't know how else to approach discipline. It's not just spanking or going into a timeout. Negative discipline can also come in the form of how to talk to our children and how we behave when they don't act the way we want.

Through this chapter, we hope to give you the information, tools, and resources necessary for you to understand positive discipline and how to build self-discipline within your child.

We completely understand that every parent has a different approach to parenting. We hope that you'll consider promoting self-discipline and using the tools for positive discipline.

Be Proactive—The Foundation for Positive Discipline

One of the most highly commended personal development books is the "7 Habits of Highly Effective People." On its own, the book offers insight and advice beyond value for any adult, but, as a parent, it's worth coming back to that first habit of "being proactive." Being proactive establishes a level of fairness in the household when it comes to living with or engaging with a toddler. Toddlers may not know much about rules and may have little respect for authority in any capacity, but they understand fairness.

So how can you be proactive and build a foundation for positive discipline?

Make very clear rules that can't fall into any other interpretation. Toddlers and young children especially like to push boundaries, and if there's an opportunity to misinterpret a rule, they'll take it. So, make very clear, understandable, and consistent rules.

Examples of these can include:

- Only nice touching
- No biting peoples
- No hitting
- No slapping
- No kicking people or animals
- Clean up before starting a new activity

Ideally, these rules won't include the word "no" or "don't," but there are only so many ways to phrase restriction on your toddler's freedom. Freedom with restrictions is the overarching concept within the Montessori Method, and you're allowing your toddler a lot of freedom, but there are restrictions. Your toddler should not inflict physical harm on you or any other living creature. Your child will eventually have to learn to clean up and a variety of other life skills.

The trick to establishing a foundation has a few core rules; ones you can always revert back to, which is why rules such as "Only nice touching," work so well. When a child does something, you have to survey only whether that was nice touching or not nice touching (kicking, biting, and so forth).

The other way that you will work proactively to build a foundation of positive discipline is to cultivate a worry-free environment. If your toddler is told "no" 50 times a day, any one of those times won't stand out more than the other 49 times they were told the word "no." However, if you have to say "no" on a rare occasion, then it is impactful.

What is Self-Discipline?

The holy grail of most productive and happy adults is that they aren't overwhelmed and overstressed Type-A people. Self-discipline is the ability and the willingness of a person to monitor and correct their own behavior. This is something that we have to learn, and it's something that our children must learn. It's not a natural feature for most people. It is also often misattributed to willpower. Self-discipline and willpower are different things. You need not teach your child to abstain or persevere for the sake of willpower training.

So, how do you teach toddlers self-discipline? Unfortunately, the best way to do it is to start removing or pulling back on things that we've enjoyed doing as parents: praise and reward. When children are told not to do something, and they face punishment, they only know not to do the thing because there's a punishment waiting. As with most things in life, the opposite is true of this initial statement. When children are told to do something, and they know there's a reward, they only do it because of the reward.

Children and toddlers build self-discipline by learning the value of doing what's right and receiving the intrinsic reward of a job well done. Eventually, your child will take their dishes to the sink, not because you told them to and then thanked them afterward, but because they know that that is the right thing to do after they finish their plate. Eventually, your toddler will know to apologize after pushing down another kid unintentionally, because it's the right thing to do. Toddlers build self-discipline through these many small acts, acknowledging when they were at fault or acting without prompting from a reward or a punishment.

A note on discipline: parents all have different ways of disciplining, but there are differences between discipline and punishment. Punishing is what it sounds like, punishing a child for unwanted behavior. Whereas discipline is upholding established rules and standards. You'll use kindness and firmness to promote self-respect, self-discipline, cooperation, problem-solving, and desired behavior. Now, it is still frustrating. A screaming toddler is a screaming toddler, and sometimes mommy or daddy need a break.

But, over time, teaching or promoting self-discipline will make day-to-day life much easier.

How can you build self-discipline?

- Pull back on your praise—say thank you only when appropriate and give very specific compliments.
- E.g., Instead of, "You're so smart," use, "You figured that out, can you show me how you did it?"
- Show interest in your child's activities without telling them they're the best thing since sliced cheese—watch them, be present, and engage in the activity with them when invited. It means more than a passive compliment.
- Provide the opportunity to make meaningful choices.
- When faced with undesired behavior, try your best not to acknowledge it or excuse yourself.
- Have high expectations.
- Say "yes" more often than "no."
- Give simple and clear directions.
- Repeat expected rules often.

When put together, these small actions or mild changes and how you interact with your toddler can have a big impact on their self-discipline.

Elements of Positive Discipline

The key elements of positive discipline revolve around responsibility, cooperation, objective thinking, respect, courtesy, honesty, and compassion. Wouldn't we all love for our toddlers to understand and employ these elements often?

But a toddler's decision-making center of the brain simply isn't developed enough to acknowledge and act in line with these elements, all the time. The best you can do to put these positive elements into play in your household is to model those behaviors.

Now, you might do that already, but your child doesn't know that. Your child doesn't have a name to give these actions, and they can't identify those actions at the moment. When do you notice there is a decision regarding responsibility, respect, honesty, or courtesy, point it out to your toddler. It can feel very self-absorbed at first, but by saying, "I opened the door for someone because it was polite," you're calling attention to that very specific action. Another example might be saying, "Dad works with your sister during playtime, and that's why they have so much fun. They cooperate."

What Happens When Children Break the Rules?

Safety is always paramount, and sometimes, you can't talk your way through rule-breaking. This goes beyond the tantrums and bleeds into running into the street, or not holding hands in a parking lot. And there's another issue with getting out of their car seat. Those snazzy busy boards help kids learn how to open snaps and clips, making them car seat Houdini's.

When a child breaks the rules, there are a few ways to handle it. If safety is a factor, then removing them from the situation is often the best initial response. There is also the option of further restrictions on freedom. For example, if your child is constantly escaping their car seat, it may not be safe to take them out as often as you might have because they've shown there's a clear pattern, they won't stay in their car seat when they need to for safety reasons. If they miss grocery trips, you might notice your toddler asking to go out with you, and then you can emphasize that they can go with you if they stay in their car seat. If they refuse to stay in their seat again, then you may choose not to take them out without help from another adult.

Biting, Scratching, Hair Pulling, and Other Physical Attacks

These issues are not as much of an emergency as they initially seem. It's developmentally appropriate. Your kid is not a bad kid, and the best approach is through proactive play. You can role-play with stuffed animals, where one stuffed animal gets hit, and the other animal says I don't like that and leaves. This is one of the few directed Montessori activities because it directly addresses how it is appropriate and respectful to touch or engage another person.

When it's directed toward you, stop their hands or feet, and say something like, "I won't let you hit me." And emphasize that hitting/kicking hurt. One of the few times that Montessori aligns with outside teaching is in these moments. Positive parenting comes from a lesson seen in the "Happiest Toddler on the Block" and focuses on Kind Ignoring.

Kind ignoring is the act of removing yourself from the situation. Now, you don't want to shame or put down the child but acknowledge that the behavior is not okay, it hurts, and you don't want it to happen to you. Acknowledge also that you will be back or available later.

Try these:

- "Mom doesn't like slaps. Mom will be back when you stop slapping."
- "Dad doesn't like bites. They hurt. Dad wants alone time because these bites hurt."
- "I don't like hits; they feel bad. I'll come back in a bit when you don't feel like hitting anymore."

These emphasize responsibility on their part and aren't a punishment, although your toddler won't feel that way. You have removed yourself from physical pain. That's not a punishment for your child, it's a relief for you.

CHAPTER 2:

Techniques Used in Positive Discipline

Technique 1: Creating Rules

Dr. Nelsen emphasizes the significance of establishing clear and reasonable rules. She recommends that as much as possible, rules are devised by children with the guidance of parents or authority figures and agreed upon by everyone. It will make them more accountable to follow the rules.

If there is a need to modify the rules or introduce a new one, make sure that your child is informed about it and understand the reasons for the modification.

Technique 2: Recognizing Needs

Another theory that governs Positive Discipline is that when the child misbehaves, he is displaying an unmet need that requires satisfaction.

It is necessary to focus on recognizing and meeting the need instead of the behavior itself to deal with the misbehavior.

Technique 3: Redirecting Negative Behavior

It is best to encourage positive behavior by redirecting the child's attention to something interesting and creative to resolve or stop the acts of misbehavior.

Technique 4: Understanding the Meaning

Sometimes, misbehavior or acting out is the child's way to get attention from his parents or other people around him. It is essential to understand that children, like adults, do not do something without a valid reason. Once you understand the trigger that caused the behavior, remove or resolve it to prevent further emotional outbursts from your kid.

Technique 5: Inspiring Intrinsic Motivation

Intrinsic motivation refers to the inherent desire of a person to feel good about oneself. The motivation comes from within and not from external sources that includes getting a reward or avoiding punishment.

All these techniques encourage the behaviors you want to see while discouraging the behaviors that you do not want to manifest in your child. In positive parenting, it is important to maintain a respectful, positive relationship with the child, while trying to decrease or increase the behavior. When things get frustrating and challenging along the way—keep your cool.

Easier said than done, right? But, when you focus on the long-term results, you will eventually say that all your efforts paid off. For now, it helps to focus on the principles of positive discipline, one day at a time. It will help you find solutions to behavioral problems, instead of temporarily stopping the problems.

The good news is—Positive Discipline is effective. Based on studies and surveys, children perform and behave better when they perceive both kindness and firmness from the parents. With high responsiveness to the feelings and needs, while setting realistic and high expectations, parents motivate children to work on concrete goals, become academically and socially successful, and less likely to engage in risky behaviors.

Discipline Strategies for Highly Sensitive Children

It has never been easy to discipline children, but it was especially difficult for parents of children with high sensitivity. Parents need to learn some tips to discipline their children effectively, especially if they are very sensitive and emotional.

One of the most gratifying jobs on the planet is being a parent, and anyone privileged to be a parent is genuinely happy. However, it isn't ever quick. Usually, hard work is the most rewarding job.

It is through this hard work that we grow up as parents and individuals and sometimes reward ourselves with those moments that hold us on our way. For a very responsive or emotional child's parents, this job will pose even more challenges.

What Are Highly Sensitive Children?

A very sensitive child is very conscious and quick to react. Feel things deeper. These children are unbelievably empathic and perceptive of their environment and how they move around in space.

When a highly vulnerable child is upset, you have to try and reassert that it's all right to get nervous and that they should retry what they've been doing if they feel a little better. These terms do not affect the child, who feels profoundly.

Now that we understand some of the elements and actions of a highly reactive child, how do parents teach and discipline? Below is a more detailed discussion of this.

How to Discipline Highly Sensitive Children

First of all, being really sensitive is not an illness or condition but a feature. Being very sensitive is a wonderful characteristic when a child and parents understand how to organize deeper emotions and feelings better.

Dismiss the Defense

As parents, our own feelings must be known. Since we detach our children from us, they are often (very often) unhappy with the decisions we make as human beings with their own emotions, feelings, and reactions. That's good.

As parents, therefore, we have to be aware and validate their own feelings. In this, it is important that we are not defensive and that we are now invaded by our emotions.

CHAPTER 3:

Getting to Know Your Young Child

Toddlers often have already developed a personality of their own. However, most parents try to override their child's personality and creativity because they feel it does not run well with their household runs. As a parent, you think you know what is best, and most of the time, you do. However, you have to understand that toddlers are becoming little people.

They have their ideas, and they are starting to think for themselves.

You must remember, your child and their feelings are valid. They are not little robots for you to order around and treat like they are supposed to be zombies. Children need support from their parents to become their person, and it starts when they are a toddler.

Of course, you want to make sure they are respectful, and a child with an attitude will need more discipline than a sweet and already obedient child; however, you do not want to disregard your toddler's mood if they have one. This is because one day, they can become a persuasive leader and very passionate. Put them on the right track to become a good leader. Do not try to squash their can-do attitude.

Listen to Them

Your child may not be the most articulate yet, but they still want you to listen to them when they talk. Children have the craziest ideas, and listening to those ideas can give you valuable insight into how their minds work. If your child is talking about something that you find impossible, don't say that. Listen to what they are saying. Let them know that it has not happened yet and that they should work on making it happen. Build them up, and don't tear them down. Even if you don't understand a word they are saying, listen to the passion in their voice. Children are the most passionate people on the planet. They have not yet hit society where power is seen as being crazy, so it is silenced. Don't stunt their love.

Believe in Them

Children are very impressionable. You could have a very outspoken and ambitious toddler that turns into a slacker as they get older. This is because someone along the way told them that they were not good enough, or that what they wanted couldn't be done. Most of the time, sadly, this is their parents. From the time they are toddlers, you should believe in them. Let them climb that rock, but be there to catch them. Let them try to read and help them. Be there to raise them and help them reach their potential. Even if you are skeptical, tell your child it is possible.

Your child will develop their personality more in their toddler years than all their years together after that.

For parents who wish for their tiny baby to stay innocent forever, life does not happen to work in their favor. Our babies rapidly morph into mini versions of us, which means an entirely different phase is in store for naïve parents. Once the walking and talking begins, there is no turning back the clock. The role of parenting becomes a whole new level of challenge, which means your life or home will never be quite the same again. Your little you are going through the physical changes and that0s why it is crucial to toddler-proof your home and life.

The toddler stage is quite a unique one during human development in the fact that toddlers are no longer considered babies but they are not considered to be preschoolers yet, either. Many crucial developmental components occur during this time frame, which is why, as parents, we should always be encouraging growth and watching for signs that our young child may be falling behind developmentally. Of course, all children learn and grow at different paces.

Gross Motor Development

Gross motor skills are physical capabilities that utilize large bodily movements that require the entire body. When your child is a toddler, they stop toddling and look so incredibly awkward when they walk. They begin to walk and can do so more smoothly. They can run and at much faster rates, as well as hop and jump. They can actively participate in throwing and catching a ball and push themselves around by themselves or while upon a riding toy.

Fine Motor Development

Slight motor movements are vastly different from gross motor skills because they require the ability to utilize precise movements to perform adequately. During the toddler stage, children can begin to create things they imagine with their own hands. They can build towers out of toy blocks, mold clay into recognizable shapes, and are more than capable of scribbling on paper with crayons or pens. They quite enjoy toys that allow them to insert specific forms into one another. This is also when parents will start to notice which hand their child prefers to use over the other, as they begin to become either right-handed or left-handed.

CHAPTER 4:

The Development of Language Activities

There are numerous approaches to draw in your baby's interest in language exercises and they will all assist in creating proper speech and language aptitudes.

If your tyke is especially in danger of building up a speech delay, it would be an extraordinary plan to incorporate some language exercises in their day by day normal as right on time as could be expected under the circumstances. Furnishing them with adoration for adapting at a convenient time will fabricate a strong establishment for their development and supply them with amusement in the meantime.

A standout amongst the best little child language exercises you can participate in is perusing. Numerous neighborhood libraries have a unique youngsters' segment where you can sit and read together. Acquiring books decreases the expense as well as empowers you to appreciate a more extensive territory than what you have close by at home. Libraries are an incredible spot to visit with your little child, and they regularly hold playgroups and early proficiency programs planned particularly for toddlers. It tends to be an unusual social activity for both you and your baby.

Another early language action includes the utilization of blaze cards. These cards use pictures and words to assist the little child with making a relationship between an article they perceive and what the spelled word resembles. Although your baby might be years from perusing, these cards can be incredible because the little child is pulled in to the hues. While you are playing with these cards, you are likewise talking with your kid. Each great language action ought to include association with the parent because the baby is showered with speech amid the procedure.

Utilizing gesture-based communication can be another extraordinary language movement for toddlers. It might appear to be contradictory to use the connection through signing to enhance speech development; however, the gesture-based interface for toddlers includes the full utilization of speech. This is an incredible action for toddlers since they are pulled in to development. Toddlers can duplicate your contact via gestures, motions, and they get immersed with a speech from the parent amid the procedure.

Other language exercises may incorporate singing. Toddlers have an incredible feeling of musicality and love to participate with tunes. It tends to be an incredible method to enable them to gain proficiency with the letters in order too.

Parent collaboration is essential for early language development, so discovering some incredible fun language exercises to do with your baby will give them a great head begin.

Tips for Buying a Toddler Bike

What kind of bicycle would you be able to get for a little child? If more established kin or companions are hustling around on "genuine" bikes, your small bright child may implore you for one of his own. You may accept that—with preparing wheels— your youngster is never unreasonably youthful for a bike. You may even trust that—with a little perseverance—you can instruct your little one to adjust without anyone else.

Before you get excessively energized, investigate your little child and think about whether your youngster is developmentally-prepared for a bicycle. As we develop from newborn children to grown-ups, our limbs become proportionally longer concerning our bodies. Most toddlers' legs are just excessively short to successfully pedal and adjust a traditional bike, an issue exacerbated by the way that they are likewise exceptionally light concerning the bicycle. Further confusing the material science is the way that those little wheels make less gyroscopic security, making it considerably harder for a bit of bike rider to remain upstanding.

When you are searching for a little child bicycle, you have likely considered purchasing a conventional accelerated bike with preparing wheels or stabilizers. Developing wheels may enable your small child to ride a motorcycle without spilling, however, making wheels present their concern in that they don't "train" anything.

Indeed, preparing wheels can make it significantly harder to figure out how to ride a two-wheel bicycle. When the equalization falls on a side preparing wheel, it is practically challenging to reestablish harmony onto the original wheels without putting a foot on the ground.

One arrangement is to leave youngsters requesting a baby bicycle on tricycles until they are mature enough to deal with and ride a proper bike appropriately. Toddlers can be persevering in their requests for a "major child bicycle."

A superior baby bicycle alternative is a stripped-down variation known as a parity bicycle: a bike without any pedals. By getting rid of pedals, a parity bicycle does not require its rider to make the troublesome change from adjusting on feet to accelerating up to a sufficiently high speed that gyroscopic solidness and instinctive directing sources of info can keep it aligned. Instead, toddlers can hurry along and lift their feet off the ground for whatever length of time that they are agreeable.

Parity bicycles enable toddlers to learn at their rate, finding the expansion in security that accompanies expanding speeds. It likewise gives them a lot of experience taking the "act of pure trust" over the moderate speed unsteadiness without focusing on falling over if they are unfit to pedal up to speed to get their parity.

An equalization bicycle is the perfect baby bicycle since it securely causes youthful youngsters to figure out how to ride a bike by adjusting first and accelerating second additionally because it would seem that a good bicycle, a parity bicycle may fulfill a baby's desire to ride like more celebrated children.

This little child bicycle can be embellished with every one of the streamers, lights, and chimes that attract toddlers to more great bikes. What's more, if youngsters spend enough riding parity bicycles, they will be prepared to adjust a genuine pedal-bicycle without making wheels when they are at long last sufficiently enormous for one!

The majority of guardians have difficulties while child-rearing their children. Numerous guardians feel especially tested with regards to the territory of child discipline.

In the zone of child discipline, guardians should be versatile, understanding, and firm when essential. Teaching a child should be age-appropriate, and in this part, we will investigate the ideal approaches to train children at the various phases of improvement.

A newborn child is reliant on guardians for everything, and the best way to convey is by crying. There are times when guardians need to practice extraordinary persistence with a youthful child who does not quit crying and does not enable their dissatisfaction to control their activities. Indeed, even at this young age, guardians need to define reasonable limits for an infant.

At the point when the child is around 6 to 9 months, it's imperative to exhibit appropriate behavior to the child and unmistakably convey what the desires are. Continuously recall that the child learns through redundancy. Indeed, even at this age, there should be consistency from guardians when encouraging schedules to children as it will enable them to comprehend what's in store. Children will emulate all that they see; thus, guardians can begin instructing them good and evil by demonstrating that behavior. At this stage redundancy, and consistency in educating schedules and displaying appropriate action is the ideal approach to train a child.

The ideal method for actualizing discipline for your children is by utilizing positive order strategies rather than negative ones. All children need endorsement and consideration; thus, guardians should offer it to them as and when they need and merit it. The order resembles instructing, and the ideal approach to encourage children is to approach discipline in a cherishing and positive manner. Toddlers need and request consideration and are at a phase where they like to test the breaking points of limits that guardians give them. The ideal approach to training a baby or preschool child is to clarify the contrast between excellent and evil and why it is critical to have discipline set up.

It is significant for guardians to be steady and firm in setting limits yet to adulate the child for good behavior. Consistency in applause and being sure when the child demonstrates ethical behavior, balanced with texture, and being firm when the child ventures over the points of confinement set by the guardians are the best method to train at this stage.

Best Toddlers Discipline Techniques for New Parents

Before we begin with the regular yet tried toddlers discipline systems to enable unseasoned parents to be ready, allow first to set up that there is nobody that perfectly fits all techniques to influencing your little ones to carry on. Every child is novel and analysts have discovered that frames of mind and propensities may in some cases be innate. What may work for one little child may not with another. Proper child-rearing abilities involve that disciplinary methods should, in this manner, be connected by a child's reaction level.

Building Solid Ground

Child-rearing tips on toddlers have one general thought with regards to little child disciplinary styles—set constraints and make the structure. Since toddlers are still reliant on their folks, the main thing you should do, particularly when your child is beginning to react adequately, is to set a daily practice.

Have your child wake up at nearly a similar time every day and make a timetable for suppers, for play, for strolling, and different exercises, so the individual in question comprehends what's in store straight away. Lucidity in regular practices is bound to deliver a polite child, compared to a baby whose day by day plan is profoundly blended and arbitrary. Try not to confine the person in question with the timetables; however; remember, this is the best age for your child to learn and investigate.

CHAPTER 5:

Understanding the Belief Behind Behavior

It's necessary for parents to bear in mind that kids are naturally good, and they have episodes of acting up due to specific reasons that they cannot voice out, especially when they are young and don't know how to process their emotions.

There are two factors behind your child's challenging behavior: the sense of not belonging (connection) and the sense of significance (contribution). When one or both basic needs are not satisfied, the children find a way to fulfill it, even if it requires adverse action. Dr. Dreikurs aptly put it by stating that "A misbehaving child is a discouraged child."

Calling the child "bad" for doing something negative isn't healthy for their self-esteem. It usually starts when your kid continually misbehaves or throw tantrums, and you are exasperated. While trying to calm them, you lose control and label them as a "bad boy" or "bad girl" unintentionally. You can forgive yourself after that little slip and quote the famous cliché that you're just human, and humans make mistakes, but if you keep repeating it every time they do something wrong, it will be engraved in their mind and damage their self-worth.

Positive discipline aims to help parents learn to objectify the behavior and cut the "bad cycle." For example, instead of telling your child when they hit their younger sibling that "that's bad" or "you're such a bad boy," you may say "it isn't okay to hit your brother when you are angry because they do not share their toy" and then let them understand the harm that might happen to their brother. When you objectify their behavior, you're teaching them the cause and effect. By directly addressing the "bad behavior" without using the term "bad," you're encouraging your child to make better choices and avoid hurting other people.

Show the child how to resolve the problem, instead of pointing out that what they did is wrong.

Redirecting your child's behavior requires more than saying, "Don't do that" or "No." It needs skills to teach them right from wrong using calm actions and words. For instance, you catch your child before they can hit their little brother, instead of saying "No hitting" or "Don't hit," tell them to "Ask their brother nicely if they want to borrow a toy." By giving them an alternative way to get the toy, you're showing them that asking is more effective than hitting.

If they already hit their brother, it's a must to be creative with your response. One right way is enforcing a non-punitive time-out, which technically is about removing the child from the stimulus that triggers their behavior and allows them to calm down. You can cuddle them when they are agitated, let them play in their room, or ask them to sit with you and read a book. After their emotion subsides, start explaining (not lecturing) why their behavior is inappropriate. Please encourage your child to give other positive options that they believe will provide them with the result they want, without hurting anyone.

Be Kind, Yet Firm When Enforcing Discipline. Show Respect and Empathy

A child may insist that what they did was right, hence the importance of enforcing safety rules and consequences to prevent similar incidents in the future. Listen to their story as to why they did it and win half the battle by displaying empathy, but still impose the consequence of their action to learn from their mistakes. Kindness makes your child feel understood, lessening their resistance, and heightened emotions.

Look for the "why" behind this behavior, especially when you observe a pattern. Sometimes, hitting a sibling is a silent message that they are jealous of the attention you're giving to the younger child. Whatever the cause, resolve the issue early to make your child feels secure and loved. Treat the root cause and not the symptoms.

Offer Choices, Whenever Possible

Giving your child positive choices works like magic when disciplining them. An example is when you're trying to make them sleep, and they still want to watch TV, instead of getting angry, provide choices. "Do you like to go to bed now or in ten minutes? Ten minutes? Okay, ten minutes and then off to bed."

This approach is a win-win solution because they get to pick the option that is okay with them, and you're offering choices that are advantageous to you. By not forcing them to do something and letting them choose, you prevent power struggle.

You allow them to take charge and show autonomy within your parameters. To successfully use this technique, provide palatably, but limited choices. Eliminate options that are not acceptable to you and honor what they select.

Use Mistakes as Learning Opportunities for Your Child

Use every misbehaving episode as a chance to learn invaluable life lessons. Often, the child misbehaves to achieve what they want or when they are bored. For instance, they throw and break toys when they do not like them anymore. Instead of scolding them, use the opportunity to teach them the idea of giving them to their friends or donating them. If they are bored, provide other exciting activities.

This will teach them the concept of displacement or finding ways to be productive and prevent their properties. By empowering them with alternatives, they will be adept at making wise choices, even if you are not with them.

Prevent the Repeat of Misbehavior by Changing the Scene

The famous adage still works—"Prevention is better than cure" in positive discipline. If you notice that your child keeps repeating an act, find ways to prevent it from recurring or resolve the problem.

One significant reason that you need to look into consideration is a transition. Most children do not like sudden changes, even in the ordinary routine. For instance, your child hates brushing their teeth in the morning and would do anything not to do it. Naturally, you will be frustrated because of the daily ordeal of resistance, which they show by crying, whining, screaming, hitting, or kicking.

What happens? It shows that they aren't resisting the act of brushing teeth; they are against the transition from sleep to a busy day because it overwhelms them. So, the next time your child repeats their tantrums over something, get to the leading cause and allows a transition time. For example, instead of rushing them to get dressed, set a timer that lets them do what they want, including getting ready. Ask him—"Do you need 20 or 30 minutes to get ready?" By letting them decide, they become in-charge of the allotted time but know that they need to show up dressed up before the time is up.

Be Clear and Consistent with Your Expectations and Boundaries

Children always find ways to push beyond the limits or find loopholes to satisfy their whims. They will attempt to test the limits to see your reaction or challenge you to know what will happen. So, it's necessary to talk to your child about the boundaries you set and the things you expect from them. Explain the corresponding consequences when they violate limits or house rules.

It is also essential to be consistent and follow through (do what you say) because it shows that you're serious about discipline. By being consistent, you're teaching them self-discipline, self-control, and other valuable lessons in life that will come in handy when they become an adult. Discipline requires a consistent application to be useful. Over time, they will recognize that their behavior and actions lead to consequences that they despise.

Use Questions, State Facts, or Single-Word Reminders, Instead of Demanding or Ordering Them to Comply

When your baby grows into a toddler, you need to find language to make them comply and cooperate. Using respectful words is essential to make them obey you without saying "Stop" and "No." Connecting with your little child requires breaking down communication barriers since they are still developing their speech skill.

It's much better to say, "Please look to your left and right before crossing the street," instead of ordering, "Don't cross the street without looking on your right and left." The word "Don't" serves as the modifier that confuses a little child. Say, for example, even if you cry out, "Don't jump in the puddle," your 2-year old kid still jumps in and wonders why you're annoyed.

Treat and talk to them like an adult. Instead of ordering them, use positive phrasing, open questions, single-word reminders, or facts.

Use, "Shall we get up now?" instead of "Time to get up!"

"Shall we put these away, so nobody trips over them?" instead of yelling, "Put them away!"

"Your face is covered with chocolate! What shall we do about it?" instead of "Wipe your face."

"Light" instead of "Turn off the light after using the toilet."

"Kind words, please." instead of "Don't speak like that."

"Water is wasting," instead of "You are wasting water."

"We need to look after your little brother," instead of "Don't hit the baby!"

How can we solve this problem?

Be generous with reasons, background information, facts, and explanations, so your child will better comprehend why they aren't allowed to do something or why they need to do it.

Involve them in problem-solving by working together as a team to find a mutually agreeable solution.

Children behave better on their free will when they see their parents as allies. By giving your child a voice and the opportunity to be heard, they become more cooperative. Brainstorm solutions together and allow them to provide suggestions on matters that ensure safety and well-being.

Allow Your Kid to Face Natural Consequences

There are two types of consequences—natural and made-up. The latter are those that you make to suit your needs and propel them to comply. Some experts say that made-up consequences are punishments in disguise.

Categorically, made-up consequences come in the forms of immediate effects, fair results, and logical development.

Immediate consequences help you teach the child to realize that their behavior is tied up with a result. An example is losing their phone privileges for a week when you find out that they are lying about getting their homework done.

Fair consequences are those that are reasonable and not overly harsh. If you ground them or prevent them from using electronics for one month, your kid would not think it's fair, and you are doing an injustice. They will fight the consequence every step of the way and try to defy it when you aren't around.

Logical consequences benefit children with specific behavior problems. An example is disallowing them to play with their toys if they refuse to put them back on the shelf. By linking the consequence with the problem, you let your child see that their choice directly results.

Natural consequences are part of natural growth. When you allow your kid to make mistakes and experience the natural results that arise from their misbehavior, you're showing them that inappropriate actions can lead them into trouble or face immediate consequences beyond your control.

For example, they touch the hot pot and get their hand burned. The pain is the natural consequence, teaching them not to do it again.

CHAPTER 6:

Understanding Age Appropriate Behavior

Children at some point in their lives misbehave, throw uncontrollable fits, display repetitive tantrums, and act out negatively. Most parents do not understand why they changed from docile and well-behaved kids into defiant ones?

Is misbehavior age-related? Is it a normal phase of growing up? Can it be prevented before its occurrence? Before exploring the many reasons why children misbehave, you need to understand the normal phase of child development.

Accordingly, each child has six domains of development which are:

1. **Physical Development**—It refers to the development and growth of his body. It includes nutrition, fitness, dental health, and general well-being.

2. **Intellectual Development**—It refers to the growth of cognitive thoughts, thought processes, and other brain functions.

3. **Language Development**—It is associated with the development of communication skills like speech, writing, body language, and reading.

4. **Emotional/Social Development**—It is about understanding oneself and others, developing self-esteem, experiencing varied emotions, as well as establishing interpersonal relationships.

5. **Moral Development**—It is the development of empathy and the child's ability to decipher right from wrong.

6. **Sexual Development**—It is the awareness of the distinct differences between male and female bodies, attitudes, and emotional responses. During the latter part of growing up, there are hormonal changes that stimulate physical desire and the capability for conception and giving birth.

Each area has a normal path of development that influences the behavior, personality, and temperament of children. Every area has a beginner, intermediate, and advanced level, the reason why some children are more capable of following rules and adapting to experiences and others are not. Once you have a solid understanding of these domains and their levels, you become adept at how to raise a well-mannered child.

Another noteworthy study is Erik Erikson's eight areas of Psychosocial Development, which are based on Sigmund Freud's theory of psychosexual development. It is focused on the resolution of issues to help children become complete, productive and successful persons. It revolves around the mastery of attitudes, skills, and ideas at every stage.

1. **Trust vs. Mistrust (From birth-12 months old)**. At this stage, infants begin to learn that adults around them can be trusted. They develop their sense of trust when their needs are met, seeing the world as a predictable and safe place. On the other hand, if the caregivers/parents are not responsive to their needs, they see the world as unpredictable, which leads to fear, mistrust, and anxiety. If they are treated with cruelty or their needs are inappropriately met, they may grow up with a sense of distrust.

2. **Autonomy vs. Doubt/Shame (From age 1-3 years old)**. Toddlers start to explore the world, act to get results and learn to control their actions. They begin to show preferences on what kind of toys, foods, or clothing they like. At this age, toddlers' main agenda is to address the issue of autonomy versus shame/doubt by establishing independence. It is the "ME DO IT" growing phase. Parents should remember that any denial of the child's input for basic decisions like choosing his clothes will impact his sense of autonomy and make him doubt his ability

to choose properly and that could lead to feelings of shame and low self-esteem.

3. **Initiative vs. Guilt (From 3-6 years old)**. During these preschool years, children become capable of asserting control and initiating activities through play and social interactions. The main task of the kids during this stage is to master the skills in achieving goals while getting along with others. When parents allow children to explore within certain boundaries and support their choices, they develop a sense of purpose and become more confident. Kids who are not successful during this stage because of over-controlling parents or bad choices may develop guilt feelings and experience deep-seated shame.

4. **Industry vs. Inferiority (From 6-12 years old)**. This is the elementary school age and the stage where children begin to face the dilemma of establishing a solid identity by exploring different roles and discovering their "adult" selves. It is an extremely critical period because it sets the path to the future. Teens who successfully adopt a positive role can remain true to their values and beliefs when facing other people's intervention, while those who struggle to establish a strong sense of identity may face a continuous struggle to "find" themselves as they go through life.

5. **Identity vs. Role Confusion (From 12-18 years old)**. This is the adolescence stage where children begin to face the dilemma of establishing a solid identity by exploring different roles and discovering their "adult" selves. It is an extremely critical period because it sets the path to the future. Teens who successfully adopt a positive role can remain true to their values and beliefs when facing other people's intervention, while those who struggle to establish a strong sense of identity may face a continuous struggle to "find" themselves as they go through life.

6. **Intimacy vs. Isolation. (From 20-early 40s)**. At this stage of early adulthood, people become concerned about personal relationships. They prepare themselves for the prospects of sharing life with others. Adults with a positive self-concept are more likely to build successful intimate relationships, while those with a weak self-concept usually experience emotional isolation and loneliness.

You may or not be around during these last stages of your child's life, but what you teach him during childhood continues to guide him through the negative issues that come up.

- **Generativity vs. Stagnation (From 40-mid 60s)**. It is middle adulthood, where people engage in productive and meaningful work to contribute to the development of others and society. This period is where adults start contributing to the next generation by giving birth (females) or caring for others. Those who fail to master the task may experience stagnation, isolation, and a sense of failure for not leaving a significant legacy in the world. Moreover, they will be disinterested in pursuing self-improvement and productivity.

- **Integrity vs. Despair (From the mid-60s to the end of life)**. It is called late adulthood, where people begin to reflect on their journey in life—either feeling a sense of satisfaction or failure. Those who are proud and satisfied with their achievements feel a strong sense of integrity and look back with few regrets. But those who are not successful in their attempts feel that their lives are wasted and look back with lots of "should have," "could have," and "would have," waiting the finality of life with feelings of despair, depression, and bitterness.

Understanding these domains and psychosocial development stages are the key tools that parents can use to help their children grow with confidence and armed with skills to gain positive outcomes from infancy to late adulthood.

Now, it's time to unlock the coded messages of misbehavior.

Why Children Misbehave?

Most often than not, children who display misbehavior are discouraged kids yearning for "significance and a sense of belonging." Social psychologist Dr. Alfred Adler affirmed in his researches that humans are naturally "hard-wired" towards these two concepts that they believe define who they are.

Positive parenting guides parents to become proactive and ready to ward off future misbehavior by meeting the emotional needs of their children. Imagine your child having two buckets—the first one is labeled Belonging and the other one is labeled Significance.

Belonging

It basically refers to a connection or how the child fits into a group (family, classroom, friends, or community). If the connection is lost, altered, or absent, this results in insecurity and other negative feelings.

You can fill up this bucket with an assurance that he plays a very important role in the family and he is loved. Spending regular time with him every day is another excellent way to fill his bucket.

Significance

It is a feeling that comes from knowing that one has contributed to the whole in a meaningful way. People feel significant when they believe that they make a difference in the group, community, or society by contributing something meaningful. Young as they are, children are also eager to contribute, cooperate, and help to solve problems through various opportunities at home or school.

You can fill up this bucket by empowering him to complete simple, age-appropriate tasks and letting him help you around. You can involve him in making meaningful decisions and choices throughout the day, making him feel valued.

It is important to remember that young kids do not have the skills to revert to the significance and belonging after feeling discouraged. They usually feel confused and mixed up, so parents should be careful when reacting to their failed attempts.

Some scenarios that display the child's attempts to reclaim significance and belonging:

- A child who feels dethroned by the arrival of the newest member of the family will show "regression" to test and explore his new role in the family. If the parent enforces a lot of time-outs as a consequence of his misbehavior, the child will interpret it as messages that he does not fit or belong in the family and he better become more creative in his "regression" acts.

- A child who receives constant criticisms or being compared to other children and made to feel inferior will stop trying and withdraw to prevent being noticed. He feels it is safer and better to pull away since he does not belong and is not perfect.

- A child who feels hurt and lonely may attempt to hurt others, so he will not be alone in his pain and misery. If the parent, teacher, or caregiver punishes him in any form, his feeling of discouragement and pain are magnified.

- A child who engages his parents or other parental figures in constant power struggles believes that it is the only way to control or be the boss. When adults fail to recognize that the child is requesting more power or control over his life and fall straight into his trap, the struggles begin.

Seeking significance and belonging can be tough even to adults. So, how do you expect growing children who are new to all these things to know the process to regain their place in the family or group where he is a member? Misbehavior is a form of communication where children speak to adults in coded messages when they suddenly feel the threats in their sense of belonging and significance.

It is vital to understand that all healthy and normal children misbehave because they are growing, exploring, discovering, learning, and experimenting. It is the duty of parents to guide, discipline, and make their journey in life more fun. You don't want to raise a grumpy child who will grow as a grumpy adult, right? So, brace yourself and become a more positive parent!

CHAPTER 7:

Emotional Factors Affecting Behavior

A child's sense of perception and reasoning is keen, but at the same time, it is fragile and easily impressionable. Just like physical factors such as sleep, hunger, and physical exertion can cause unfavorable behavior changes, so can emotional or psychological factors. Things that can scar, hurt, frighten, or threaten a child's sensibilities are bound to leave lasting impressions on the child's behavior.

Children have attack and defense mechanisms to counter what they consider a threat or overcome what scares them. We shall look at a few such things that are the most common factors observed that can change a child's conduct.

Insult and Fear

Kids have a very delicate sense of self-respect and honor. A ridiculing comment, even by a well-meaning parent, about a child's work of art, for example, can seriously hurt a child. Cases of kids feeling insulted and humiliated so much that it affects their behavior are seen more in kindergarteners or kids of any school age. Kids starting preschool or kindergarten are exposed to different kids from various households, causing kids to defy around them emotionally. If the accompanying kids do not feel like threats, these defenses might well dissolve. But, insulting talk, laughter at each other's expense can often cause such kids to strengthen their emotional walls. These can very well carry back to the child's own home. Suppose they cannot communicate or unwilling to disclose what happened at school or the park to upset their disposition. In that case, this frustration and sense of humiliation will stay bottled up. This can cause kids to develop an inferiority complex and a deficient level of self-worth.

This was just one factor of feeling insulted. Perhaps, a different side of the same coin is fear. Feeling threatened by situations, intimidating adults, or even bullying school mates, can severely scar a child's innocent mind. This particular factor is wider, seeing as a child can feel scared or threatened by many things. A menacing-looking man at a grocery store, a ferocious dog at a park or in a neighbor's yard, can considerably frighten a young mind, making a child feel threatened.

One of the most common consequences of feeling either scared or insulted is seeing a downturn in a child's health. The two most common ailments that young children suffer from are an upset stomach or the common cold with cough. There is a noticeable relation between these ailments and kids undergoing some traumatic experience, either a humiliation (for cases of a stomach ache) or fear of some kind (for insistent bouts of cold and cough). It stands to reason then that we don't just have emotional sensibilities and the resulting behavioral changes but also our kids' very health when faced with emotionally stressful situations.

All kids are different, and their reactions to different situations are equally as diverse. How one kid reacts to a threat might be entirely different from how another child would respond. What might be a situation of utter panic and fear for one could be a chance to prove themselves and step on the other's offensive? Their innate temperaments, mental constitutions, their environment at home, and interactions within the family, and their observations and inferences of the world around them will add to how kids would potentially react to stressful situations. An only child, or a first-born, or a highly pampered, overly protected, and doted-upon child, will undoubtedly be scared, feeling lonely, and exposed when confronting an intimidating scenario. Whereas, a child who has seen brothers and sisters fight, seen their siblings come back from school after an argument, or any such other exposure, would be at least a bit better prepared for any unpleasant situation outside of their homes.

Withdrawing oneself in a shell, going quiet and inexpressive, being secretive about even simple day-to-day activities are only a few possible changes observed in a child feeling scared or bullied. A decrease in self-worth, low self-confidence, and a strong sense of inferiority can be seen in a child who is always made fun of, even if the joke is small. If it happens enough, it has the potential to scar a child's confidence permanently.

What Can We Do?

Talk about it. We can and must talk even before we see signs of emotional stress in our kids, but more so if we see such signs. Establishing a trusting and friendly relationship with your child is essential. Your child must not hesitate to come to you and relieve their emotional burdens at your feet when they face a problem. It would help if you were their first choice of a confidant. Are you there at the top of the list of their best friends? If not, there is a need for you to work on your trust-acquiring skills. Whether your child is facing bullying at school or constantly insulting jibes from a mean cousin, you must become the first person your child turns to. Talking is your tool to gain their trust. Talk with them to lift their spirits, to restore their confidence, and to help them see themselves in a better light.

Make sure to keep your comments and observations genuine. Fake praises and false encouragement would cause more harm than benefit. It would hurt their self-respect more to find that your words and talk weren't honest. For those kids who are struggling with fear, you must talk to them to gain their faith to share their worries with you. It would help if you were a pillar of strength and security for them. Please take steps to ensure their fears are taken care of. Enquire into situations or about persons that scare them and work toward addressing the issue. If they can witness you standing up for them and removing things that scare them, it will strengthen your bond. And this is always a good thing.

Wishes and Wants

Unfulfilled emotional needs and desires are the most significant factors to affect a child's behavior. These are extensive parameters with a broad scope of what can fall in between. From basic and vital needs to the most trivial and silly wishes, kids can get affected by them. Depending on age, such unfulfilled needs can cause slight to severe changes in their behavior in kids. For kids, things like needing a hug, wanting a new toy, or a pat on the back, are all personal wishes and wants even though their path to fulfillment is physical.

One must tread carefully when dealing with a child's emotions. An adult might not understand the significance of wanting to go to the park, ice cream at an ungodly hour or take the dog out for a walk in the middle of the night. What seems silly, laughable, and downright humorous for an adult can be a huge deal in a child's eyes. Children can quickly become stubborn, unreasonable, and throw one tantrum after another if their wishes aren't fulfilled. So how do we understand what the child needs, why it's important to them, and how to fulfill or deny their want in a harmless way?

While dealing with a stubborn child wishing for something impossible, it is essential to keep the child's age in mind and remember the three age groups and our supposed focus for each of them. For kids under three, your attention, love, and care in the world for them. There is hardly room for rules or discipline. For kids of this age group, you must deal with the utmost love and care in handling their wishes. Try diverting their minds to more plausible options for entertainment or games, or some such distraction far off the subject. Though these wishes can cause displays of stubborn behavior, there are chances of far more permanent effects of such unfulfilled desires. Improper handling can cause kids to develop spite toward the adults dealing with them. Many older kids have also been known to turn revengeful when their wishes aren't met. All this can be avoided and resolved by using the right technique while handling a tantrum.

Kids live in a constant stream of observing, learning, and adopting scenarios. It is reasonable to understand that when a four-year-old watches his younger brother playing with a toy and wishing he had this toy, what he feels within is a mixture of jealousy, anger, and resentment. Mild reflections of all these emotions, for someone so young, but they are there. You deny your child extra TV time, and he throws the cushion across the hall; what he is feeling is anger. Kids do not know what these emotions are called. There is always a new emotion for them that comes to the fore in different situations. If you can establish a connection with your child early on, then you can help him calm these new emotions and experiences and get him to label them appropriately.

One might argue as to how naming emotions could benefit kids. For one thing, your kid's emotional range is expanded, and he or she can acknowledge it, and more importantly, a child recognizes the emotions to stay away from along with being able to identify these emotions when present in others. It helps them decide which emotions are safe to hold on to and explore, and which ones are to be rid of for maintaining a healthy mind. It contributes to the overall growth of the child as a sensitively alert person.

CHAPTER 8:

Effective Communications

Being able to effectively communicate with your child means that you are able to understand their calls for different needs and responding to those calls with an appropriate response. Doing this begins right from the age of infancy. It is nothing new for a parent to recognize, acknowledge, and answer these calls right from the time of birth. Babies cry and whine along with giving any number of cues to a parent for their many needs, from hunger or sleep to discomfort or needing to be held.

Most parents are adept at recognizing these signs and responding to them appropriately. Even before the child is able to talk, they try and communicate with the help of cues. Cues such as pointing to a certain object when they need something, a bottle of juice perhaps, or holding up their hands when they need to be held, are common with kids who are yet unable to talk. It is important that a parent or caregiver acknowledges these cues and responds accordingly.

Using Appropriate Nomenclature

It is important that parents and kids resort to using proper names for their day-to-day used objects. Making a habit of using proper names for items regularly used goes a long way in ensuring that your child learns them quickly, and this makes for swifter communications. Using correct names for everyday items encourages a child to learn them faster and use them correctly.

Avoid Baby Talk

The child might not yet know how to pronounce a certain word and might begin calling it by their own equivalent that might have a similar sound or a combination of similar sounding letters. For example, a child who wishes to say "juice," might instead say "ja-ju." This is fine, and while the child will learn to say juice over time, you can help them learn faster by saying "juice" and avoiding using "ja-ju" for juice yourself. When parents use baby talk for different things to communicate with the child, it delays the learning curve of the child. Always try and use the proper names for objects and encourage your child to learn this way.

Respecting Your Child

Begin respecting your child early on. Even when they are young and unable to talk and communicate using words, make it a point to give them importance in interactions and include them whenever possible.

For example, if you are feeding your child, you could include your child in the activity by saying something like, "Would you like to hold this spoon while mommy feeds you?"

Or if you are giving your child a bath and you recite rhymes while doing so as a bath-time-play, you could ask your child what rhyme they wish for and you could both sing that together. The point here is to make the child feel valued, included, and respected.

We want them to understand and believe that their choices and opinions matter to us and we are ready to hear them out. It is essential that you begin to inculcate this feeling as early as you can. Being valued and validated goes a long way in incorporating confidence in kids from an early age.

Expressing Emotions

Kids being able to express their emotions efficiently is an important part of having effective communication. But to do this, they would need our loving guidance to show them what it is that they are feeling. A parent can help their child in this regard by helping them name the emotion they are feeling.

For example, if you notice your child sitting quietly after they have just waved goodbye to their grandparents, you could say something like, "I understand you must be sad because grandma left for her trip. Are you missing her already? It's ok to be sad."

Or something like, "You are pounding the table, you must be angry."

What this practice does is it gives a name to what they are going through or the feeling they are experiencing. This is extremely helpful when you would like to teach them how to react or behave when they experience a similar feeling again in the future.

For example, you wish to tell your child that they ought to look at positive or brighter things when they are sad. But to do this, they would have to know what being sad is in the first place. Like when their grandma has gone for the trip, you would want them to look at the brighter side of things with something like, "You can make a welcome back card for her when she comes back." Or when your child is angry, you might want to say, "Take a deep breath three times when you are angry." Only when your child is able to relate the name of the emotion to what they felt when they experienced it themselves will they be able to grasp and put your advice into practice.

Naming emotions is also essential when you want to teach your child what emotions are fine to express, and which should be controlled.

Positive Talk

Another important pillar to excellent communication with kids, especially in the toddler age, is to use positive talk. This is when what you say consists of what the child can, should, or must do instead of what they can't, shouldn't, or mustn't do.

Avoiding Negatives

Make it a habit to talk to your child in positive sentences. When you know that what you are going to say will involve a negation or denial of some kind, use a positive alternative to it in its place. A straight out "no" is more difficult for a toddler to process than a positive alternative. Consider the following dialog between a toddler and a parent.

Child: Can we go to the park today?

Parent: No, not today.

Child: Why not today? I want to go now! I am bored.

Parent: I told you not today. Go play with your toys now.

This scenario can quickly escalate into a tantrum or even a meltdown. Now see the same dialog without the negatives.

Child: Can we go to the park today?

Parent: I think we'll go to the park tomorrow.

Child: But I am bored now!

Parent: How about we both play with your toys now and we go to the park tomorrow?

You see that the child refrains from asking, "Why not today?" in the second scenario because the parent hasn't really said, "Not today." Instead, they used a positive alternative. Also, it is important to notice that the parent has involved the child to validate their reasoning and choice of activity, along with offering to play with them themselves. It is an important approach to be mindful of.

Using "no" frequently to answer your child's requests and wishes can turn them bitter from within. It generates a feeling of being denied time and again when faced with an outright no. Instead, if the same is relayed using a positive alternative, it doesn't have the same drastic effects and is more encouraging and confidence-building for the child.

Reframing

Also important is to avoid a constant barrage of negative instructions. If a child is used to hearing things like, "don't do this," "don't do that," on a regular basis, this can only sow resentment in the child's mind toward the parent. And that is not something a parent would ever want. See the following example to understand the scenario better.

If your child is running around in the house or jumping on the sofa, you are bound to say something like don't run, and don't jump. Instead, you could simply reframe the sentences to avoid the negative and say something like, "We should walk inside the house. You may run when outside in the garden or the park," and "We jump on the ground and sit on the sofa."

You could even attach a line of caution with respect to values you follow at home or about their own safety that might be at stake due to their actions. But never begin your instruction or advice with a negative. Give up using "don't" in such situations.

Doing this ensures your child doesn't feel restricted or denied simple pleasures constantly.

Practical Strategies for Effective Communication

There are a few actionable points that you can make use of and put into practice when you wish to communicate with your child with ease and efficiency. Keeping these tips in mind will help you talk in a manner that your child can easily understand and, at the same time, accept what you are saying for the value it carries. You will be able to reach your child more effectively this way.

Maintaining Eye Level

Always make it a point to talk to your kids when you are at their level. Get down, either on your knees or with your back bent, so you are on the same level with your child. Being on the same level as them is similar to taking them into confidence before saying anything. This simple step makes you more approachable and easier to understand. Even if what you are saying is not of an intimidating nature, your straight and unyielding stance can make it appear to be so. Therefore, it is always a good idea to talk to kids when at their same level. Also, when they are talking, and you are simply listening, being on their level shows interest on your part, and your child would, therefore, be more willing to talk and open up to you this way.

Affirm and Repeat

When your child is trying to tell you something, either through words, fully framed sentences, or just gestures and cues, it is always advisable to affirm their thoughts out loud. Repeat after them to let them know you are listening to them and are ready to hear them out and understand their needs or wishes. This is especially true in the case of younger kids of around two years who have just begun to talk. This can also help you understand them better when all you have are a few broken words or gestures to go on. Affirming their opinions and repeating after them gives them a chance to acknowledge if what you have understood is indeed what they have been trying to say or deny and alter their approach to help you understand better.

For example, "You are pointing at that teddy, do you wish to play?", or

"I understand you want to have ice cream but let's have it together after dinner."

Parental Narratives

Narratives are when you involve your child in your day-to-day activities by talking to them about the work you are doing or telling them a story of your past or some hilarious anecdote from your childhood. The point here is to talk to them and make them feel involved. These simple narrations can help establish an atmosphere of ease around your child and help them be confident about opening up to you in a similar way when they need to. It also gives them a sense of importance to know that you think them important enough to share such things with them, and they will be more willing to reciprocate in the future.

For example, if you are making an omelet and your child is sitting at a table near you, just talk to them about what you are doing in a simple narrative. Or you could talk to them about an omelet related story from your childhood. Making them feel involved and valued is the key.

CHAPTER 9:

Building Confidence for Kids

Confidence is fundamental for a kid to create in the beginning phases of their life. It is essential since it is expected to conquer numerous snags that your youngster will look for throughout everyday life. It is the activity of the parent of the youngster to enable the kid to manufacture fearlessness. There is a wide range of ways that you can boost your youngster to assemble certainty.

Building your youngster's fearlessness won't just cause them to feel great about themselves yet additionally set them up for the future also. You may end up asking, what would I be able to do to give my kid higher self-assurance? The appropriate response isn't confounded, and indeed, there are a few things you can do day by day that will help, and they will take a couple of moments.

The accompanying book will give you some accommodating data on the significance of building self-assurance and how to do it as such. Guaranteeing that you give close consideration and take in all the data and manufacture your youngster's certainty will be a lot simpler errand.

The Basics

On the off chance that you are new to child-rearing, there are presumably numerous things that you are not so much sure about how to do. One of these things might be how fundamental structure trust in your kid is or how to assemble trust. Try not to stress; only like each other test you have looked at in your life, it is attainable. Everything you have to do is gain proficiency with some supportive strategies and put in a safe spot some additional time for your kid, and building their fearlessness will be as simple as a stroll in the recreation center.

An individual's certainty levels as a grown-up are altogether affected by the degree of certainty that they had as a kid. This is one of the principal reasons why it is crucial to such an extent that you ingrain a reliable measure of trust into your youngster. With a tad of exertion and time, your youngster will, without a doubt, build up this significant fundamental ability.

There are a couple of things that, as a parent, you should do. Coming up next are a few models:

Continuously Make Time

You should consistently set aside a few minutes for your youngster, regardless of how bustling you are! Demonstrating that your kid precedes everything else is a brilliant method of building a kid's fearlessness and self-esteem. It is encouraged to require some investment to plan exercises with your youngster that can help make their certainty. This could be taking them to accomplish something they are acceptable at or perhaps taking them to take a stab at something new. This will give them that they are skilled, which is an excellent certainty promoter. One model could be taking a kid to the recreation center for a round of ball. On the off chance that your kid isn't into sports, take them to an occasion that will permit them to show their insight on things and consistently show how intrigued you are.

Try not to Be Too Hard

Although it is fundamental not to be excessively straightforward on your youngster, it is likewise significant not to be overly rigid. Being too simple on your kid will probably not impart legitimate ethics in a youngster or instruct them to be capable; then again, being too cruel will likely prompt low fearlessness because a kid will feel as though they do nothing right. You, as a parent, must locate the center ground and be equivalent to your order. Only one out of every odd kid will react to a similar sort of child-rearing, so it is essential to trial and see what works best regarding building your kid's confidence.

Be a Positive Example

It is your activity as a parent to set a positive model for your youngster and be a good example. One of the character qualities that your youngster will probably gain from you is your degree of self-assurance. It would help if you consistently showed up as though you have a circumstance leveled out and trust yourself. Additionally, never talk contrarily about yourself before your kid since this will probably make them build up a similar propensity.

Watch Out for Bullies

Tormenting is getting progressively better known. This is likely coming from the way that children can menace each other whenever and wherever because of web-based media. Tormenting is most likely probably the snappiest way a kid's self-assurance can be obliterated. Menaces frequently experience the ill effects of low trust in themselves to cause themselves to feel better; they attempt to bring down others' confidence.

This is why you should keep an eye out for your youngster's signs of being harassed and put an immediate end to it! A couple of instances of practices your youngster may display while being driven are:

- Suddenly no longer needs to go to class
- Depression
- Anxiety
- Fear
- Less Social Interactions
- Not appearing Themselves
- Not Wanting to Talk About Their School Day

If you notice any of these signs, you have to make a prompt move!

Show That You Believe in Them

The following stage that we will connect with for making trust in your kid is telling your kid that you have faith in them. This is a straightforward undertaking to do and requires little exertion. In any case, it is as yet essential. There are various ways that you can tell your kid you trust in them. With enough effort and time, you will have the option to discover exercises that essentially improve your youngster's confidence while demonstrating that you have confidence in them.

Numerous individuals might be uncertain of how to successfully play out this progression and might not have thought of where to start. Is it accurate to say that you are one of these individuals? If the appropriate response is right, don't stress, youngsters don't accompany manuals, yet you can get counsel from this book.

Tips to Assist You in Building Your Youngster's Self-Confidence

The way toward demonstrating to your youngster that you trust in them can be finished from multiple perspectives. Frequently, what works for one youngster won't have a similar effect on another. This implies you will probably need to attempt different things until you discover something that works. If you don't have the foggiest idea where to begin, a couple of models are given underneath:

Urge Your Child to Try New Things

Urging your youngster to attempt new things is a fantastic method of building their confidence and giving them that you ultimately put stock in their capacities to achieve something. Kindly focus on what your kid lets you know, particularly regarding what they might want to do yet don't feel that they would be any acceptable at it. Utilize this circumstance as an approach to show that you trust in them by urging them to attempt. Disclose to them that you think in them and that they can do anything they set their focus on.

It is necessary to clarify that they may not be incredible when they were first beginning, yet after some time and with training, they will show signs of improvement.

Push Them Out of Their Comfort Zone

At the point when youngsters are stuck in a safe place, their odds of building their self-confidence are a lot slimmer than that of a kid who is continually testing themselves. Training your youngster to challenge themselves will fundamentally improve their fearlessness while simultaneously giving them that you accept that they can do anything.

Recognition Their Achievements

They recognize your youngster's feelings of trepidation, just as their accomplishments, are imperative in the job of helping your kid build up a substantial degree of self-assurance. This is particularly evident when a youngster wins over their dread to achieve something. It is critical to remember that while attempting to construct a youngster's confidence, every single achievement ought to be noted. Regardless of how little the undertaking is, your kid will incredibly profit by you recognizing their accomplishment.

We will go over the significance of and the approaches to applaud a youngster's accomplishments first.

Acclaim Their Achievements

Applauding your youngster's accomplishments, regardless of how little it might appear to you, is essential during making certainty. This will cause your youngster to feel great about themselves and will likewise produce fearlessness since they will feel as though they are persistently doing things that intrigue you.

Commending your kid's accomplishments can have more sure results than ceaselessly calling attention to your youngster's negative things. This isn't unexpected since continually bringing up an inappropriate something a kid causes them to feel like they can't do anything right. Then again, continually adulating your youngster's accomplishments and not conversing with them about slip-ups generates unfriendly results. This is because the youngster will feel as though they can do anything incorrectly. It is necessary to locate a stable harmony between calling attention to botches and commending accomplishments.

While lauding your kid's accomplishments, you should be mindful of ruining or over-treat them. If you furnish your kid with a massive prize each time, they complete a little undertaking, they will generally start to feel that this will happen each time they accomplish something. This can prompt harmful practices when the prizes stop as the kid will be confounded regarding why they no longer get an award for a specific errand. It is encouraged that awards be put aside for huger achievements. Regarding littler accomplishments, verbal acknowledgment or a gesture of congratulations will get the job done fine and dandy.

Comprehend Your Child's Fears

Understanding your kid's feelings of trepidation likewise assumes an enormous job in the improvement of your kid's self-assurance. You might be asking, by what method fear can make my kid more positive about themselves. The appropriate response is the way that beating apprehension can help an individual's self-assurance drastically. While attempting to conquer fears, it is fundamental that you initially get them.

You would prefer not to set your kid up for disappointment. A portion of the things they might be terrified to endeavor might be excessively hard for them. One of the most noticeably awful things you can do while attempting to fabricate a youngster's confidence is to place them in a circumstance where they won't win. You have to converse with your kid and find what it is that they fear endeavoring and decide whether it would be a smart thought to push your kid toward confronting those feelings of trepidation.

Conclusion

Thank you for reading this book until the end. I hope that it inspires and guides you on your parenting journey.

Parenting is about providing loving guidance with great purpose—to mold the character and personality of your child. It is about understanding who he is, what he cares about, what his dreams are, what brings him happiness or sadness, and what are his strengths and weaknesses. It is about focusing your time and attention on what matters to him while keeping limitations and boundaries.

Parenting is also learning about yourself as a nurturer, a disciplinarian, a confidant, and many other roles associated with it. If you make mistakes or feel your patience running out, take a time-out, and relax. You become a fine parent when you are happy, calm, and centered. Your health and well-being matter because it helps you become an objective, affectionate, and positive parent.

Training kids with positive discipline and giving them a perfect code of living is not an easy task at all. Every kid is different from the other and they have their own understanding of the events as well, although there are some set patterns defined that parents make kids learn. But, the self-understating and evaluation of the matters cause a real difference in their understanding and practice.

As parents, it is important to understand that all kids are different and have different needs or interests. You can make them learn some of the basic things like personal hygiene, mannerism, understanding of world order, and basic behaviors in general. However, it is not possible to control their reactions, emotions, actions, and understanding about everything that is around them.

There should be mutual interests and consultation but the liberty of selection. Your kids need ultimate help from you in the hard times. Their attitude and behavior ask you to look at them and ask the matter not to just punish and put them in detention. You can identify the important needs of your child and evaluate when, how you can help them with the question, issues, and problems they have. Additionally, you can reconnect them to the humankind and reality of life by cutting them off from the imaginary world of cartoons. Overall, your combined efforts of good food, lifestyle, education, time, money, and support can lead the kids to positive discipline in life.

Finally, I wish you good luck for being a wonderful parent who believes that you need tools and guides to bring out the best in your child.